To Elisabeth,

Affirmations for Positivity, Self-Love and Confidence

Thank you for your fab energy.

By Elroy 'Spoonface' Powell

Spoon The Voice Guy

on wards + up

SPoon

April 2021

Affirmations for Positivity, Self-Love and Confidence

Copyright 2021 FAADA LTD, 1st Floor, 85 Great Portland St. London W1W 7LT, UK

http://spoon.house
info@thesuccesstips.com
thesuccesstips.com
http://r4dstore.com

ISBN 978-1-8383708-4-8 (Paper Back)
ISBN 978-1-8383708-5-5 (Kindle)
ISBN 978-1-8383708-6-2 (Audible)

Published by FAADA
Author & Editor: Elroy 'Spoonface 'Powell
@spoonface1

Disclaimer

Affirmations for Positivity, Self-Love and Confidence is intended for information purposes only.

The information provided is not intended to be a substitute for professional medical advice, diagnosis or treatment.

The Editor, Author, Publisher and Resellers accept no responsibility for loss, damage or injury to persons or their belongings as either a direct or indirect result of reading this book.

By listening to the audio versions, using our programs, services and/or products, you are agreeing to accept all parts of this disclaimer. Thus, if you do not agree to the disclaimer, please stop using it now.

Always consult your physician **before** beginning any **exercise** program.

We have made every attempt to locate the copyright holders of the additional material available and we will amend any future revisions of this book if new information arises.

Affiliate Link Disclaimer

This book contains affiliate links, which means that if you click or otherwise use one of the product links, we'll receive a small commission. This helps support the project and allows us to continue to make books and other content like this. Thank you for the support!

Table of Contents

Gratitude

What are affirmations?

How to use these affirmations

Affirmations for Positive Thinking and Confidence

Affirmations for Self-worth and Inspiration

Affirmations for Acceptance and Prosperity

How to make Your Own Affirmations

Notes

References

Gratitude

Gratitude can release us from our perceived negative emotions.

It can also reinforce generous behaviour, release endorphins and help us recognise our worth.

It has a lasting effect on the brain, making us feel better for longer.

When we feel gratitude, the ventral and dorsal medial pre-frontal cortex are activated. These areas are involved in the feelings of reward (the reward when we remove stress), positive social interactions, bonding and the ability to understand others.

—

Thank you, universal energy.

Thank you, Mama Rose and Jen Jen.

Mama Rose for the inspiration as I see how gratitude fuels your spirit and Jen Jen for the love that we share that excites us into giving.

Thank you to my Ready For Dreams and Insight Timer community.

Thank you all.

What are affirmations?

Affirmations are positive motivational sentences. They are small statements you can listen to and/or say to yourself. With consistency, they enter your subconscious and, coupled with action, they can help you feel better or achieve a specific goal.

Our brains are wired for survival and we can often perceive danger where it doesn't 'really' exist to keep us safe and in a place of 'least resistance'.

The National Science Foundation ran a study that suggested, on average, that a person has about 12,000 to 60,000 thoughts per day. Of those, 80% are negative and 95% are repetitive.

Affirmations can help us flood our minds with positive thoughts and start to believe them.

I believe the aim is not to actually erase all negative thoughts. Some of them may actually be useful. I feel that it simply helps to become aware, to explore the origins of the fear, to let go of the unnecessary, and to heal and install new thoughts that serve us better.

How to use these affirmations

1.

Decide on the reason for using these affirmations in the first place.

This can be as part of your own practice, for general maintenance or for accelerated results.

Affirmation Accelerator

For accelerated results, try reading for a minimum 1 - 10 mins twice a day.

For a 30-day detox

Read one each day for 30 days.

For a Mindful Moment in your day or week

Read any affirmation of your choice as and when you need it.

There are no rules. Have fun and find what works for you.

2.

Get comfortable. Prepare your environment inside and out for comfort and openness.

3.

Recognise the power you have to make the choices you are making and connect with a sense of gratitude.

4.

Breathe and find a balance of the elements that work for you.

5.

Would you like me to read your affirmations for you?

Get in touch.

Social media - @spoonface1

Email - info@thesuccesstips.com

Affirmations for Positive Thinking and Confidence

I am grateful for all I have and all I am.

I am grateful for all I have and all I am.

I am grateful for all I have and all I am.

I exist in my highest power and grow stronger every day.

I exist in my highest power and grow stronger every day

I exist in my highest power and grow stronger every day.

My ability to give and receive love is infinite.

My ability to give and receive love is infinite.

My ability to give and receive love is infinite.

I have an abundance of inner peace and let go of what doesn't serve me.

I have an abundance of inner peace and let go of what doesn't serve me.

I have an abundance of inner peace and let go of what doesn't serve me.

There is no space in my life for negativity.

There is no space in my life for negativity.

There is no space in my life for negativity.

I rise above and conquer all challenges.

I rise above and conquer all challenges.

I rise above and conquer all challenges.

I forgive myself and have permission
to claim all that truly nurtures and brings me joy.

I forgive myself and have permission
to claim all that truly nurtures and brings me joy.

I forgive myself and have permission
to claim all that truly nurtures and brings me joy.

I choose to reclaim my energy and live stress free.

I choose to reclaim my energy and live stress free

I choose to reclaim my energy and live stress free.

I am worthy of the opportunities presented to me and embrace them wholeheartedly.

I am worthy of the opportunities presented to me and embrace them wholeheartedly.

I am worthy of the opportunities presented to me and embrace them wholeheartedly.

I choose my family and decide my inner circle.

I choose my family and decide my inner circle.

I choose my family and decide my inner circle.

I believe in my skills and trust my abilities.

I believe in my skills and trust my abilities.

I believe in my skills and trust my abilities.

I am in the best health inside and out.

I am in the best health inside and out.

I am in the best health inside and out.

My will is unbreakable and I am unstoppable.

My will is unbreakable and I am unstoppable.

My will is unbreakable and I am unstoppable.

I have focus, clarity and indomitable spirit.

I have focus, clarity and indomitable spirit.

I have focus, clarity and indomitable spirit.

I create my own reality
and receive what I ask of the universe with ease.

I create my own reality
and receive what I ask of the universe with ease.

I create my own reality
and receive what I ask of the universe with ease.

I love myself.

I love myself.

I love myself.

I choose to let go of what I can't control and live stress free.

I choose to let go of what I can't control and live stress free.

I choose to let go of what I can't control and live stress free.

I am full of passion and overflow with joy.

I am full of passion and overflow with joy.

I am full of passion and overflow with joy.

I am worthy of love, joy and freedom.

I am worthy of love, joy and freedom.

I am worthy of love, joy and freedom.

I learned from my experiences and heal every day.

I learned from my experiences and heal every day.

I learned from my experiences and heal every day.

I am worthy of all the gifts the universe has given me.

I am worthy of all the gifts the universe has given me.

I am worthy of all the gifts the universe has given me.

I have the power of choice and step with joy into my destiny.

I have the power of choice and step with joy into my destiny.

I have the power of choice and step with joy into my destiny.

I choose my definition of success and the tools are in my possession.

I choose my definition of success and the tools are in my possession.

I choose my definition of success and the tools are in my possession.

My every desire is achievable.

My every desire is achievable.

My every desire is achievable.

I believe in me.

I believe in me.

I believe in me.

The more I give, the more I receive.
The more I receive, the more I give.

The more I give, the more I receive.
The more I receive, the more I give.

The more I give, the more I receive.
The more I receive, the more I give.

Affirmations for Self-worth
and Inspiration

I am grateful for all I have and all I am.

I am grateful for all I have and all I am.

I am grateful for all I have and all I am.

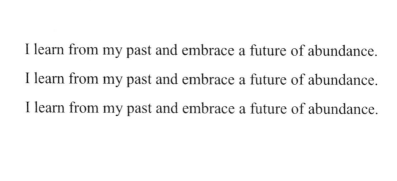

I learn from my past and embrace a future of abundance.

I learn from my past and embrace a future of abundance.

I learn from my past and embrace a future of abundance.

I am worthy of greatness.

I am worthy of greatness.

I am worthy of greatness.

I trust my skills and experience.

I trust my skills and experience.

I trust my skills and experience.

I forgive myself.

I forgive myself.

I forgive myself.

I give myself permission.

I give myself permission.

I give myself permission.

I create solutions, freedom and peace.

I create solutions, freedom and peace.

I create solutions, freedom and peace.

I resonate in my highest self and inspire joy wherever I go.

I resonate to my highest self and inspire joy wherever I go.

I resonate to my highest self and inspire joy wherever I go.

I trust my unique approach to life.

I trust my unique approach to life.

I trust my unique approach to life.

I love the positive impact of my actions.

I love the positive impact of my actions.

I love the positive impact of my actions.

I let go of pleasing people
and embrace the power of my authenticity.

I let go of pleasing people
and embrace the power of my authenticity.

I let go of pleasing people
and embrace the power of my authenticity.

I serve with love and avoid depletion.

I serve with love and avoid depletion.

I serve with love and avoid depletion.

I am financially free and at my best from the inside out.

I am financially free and at my best from the inside out.

I am financially free and at my best from the inside out.

My business is successful and in high demand.

My business is successful and in hard demand.

My business is successful and in high demand.

I create my own definition of success.

I create my own definition of success.

I create my own definition of success.

I am winning.

I am winning.

I am winning.

I am winning.

I am winning.

Affirmations for Acceptance
and Prosperity

I am love and I am loved.

I am love and I am loved.

I am love and I am loved.

I am worthy of the love I receive.

I am worthy of the love I receive.

I am worthy of the love I receive.

I forgive myself.

I forgive myself.

I forgive myself.

Forgiveness sets me free.

Forgiveness sets me free.

Forgiveness sets me free.

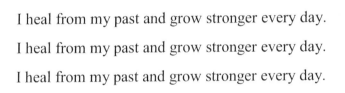

I heal from my past and grow stronger every day.

I heal from my past and grow stronger every day.

I heal from my past and grow stronger every day.

I embrace my tears as healing fuel for my soul.

I embrace my tears as healing fuel for my soul.

I embrace my tears as healing fuel for my soul.

I lift my inner child with love and forgiveness.

I lift my inner child with love and forgiveness.

I lift my inner child with love and forgiveness.

I embrace the lessons of my shadow and expand into my greatness.

I embrace the lessons of my shadow and expand into my greatness.

I embrace the lessons of my shadow and expand into my greatness.

I am grateful for the love that surrounds me.

I am grateful for the love that surrounds me.

I am grateful for the love that surrounds me.

I own my actions and flourish.

I own my actions and flourish.

I own my actions and flourish.

My growth and vitality is limitless.

My growth and vitality is limitless.

My growth and vitality is limitless.

I am open to receive in abundance.

I am open to receive in abundance.

I am open to receive in abundance.

I rise into the abundant glow of my prosperity

I rise into the abundant glow of my prosperity.

I rise into the abundant glow of my prosperity.

My inner peace gives me comfort and serves me through the storms.

My inner peace gives me comfort and serves me through the storms.

My inner peace gives me comfort and serves me through the storms.

I give without depleting and receive with abundance.

I give without depleting and receive with abundance.

I give without depleting and receive with abundance.

I radiate love from the inside out.

I radiate love from the inside out.

I radiate love from the inside out.

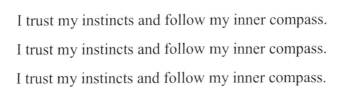

I trust my instincts and follow my inner compass.

I trust my instincts and follow my inner compass.

I trust my instincts and follow my inner compass.

I am strong. I am bold. I step into my highest power.

I am strong. I am bold. I step into my highest power.

I am strong. I am bold. I step into my highest power.

I celebrate the new choices I make from the lessons of my past.

I celebrate the new choices I make from the lessons of my past.

I celebrate the new choices I make from the lessons of my past.

I love myself without comparison.

I love myself without comparison.

I love myself without comparison.

I create my own definition of success and achieve it every day.

I create my own definition of success and achieve it every day.

I create my own definition of success and achieve it every day.

I am energised and laser-focused.

I am energised and laser-focused.

I am energised and laser-focused.

My endeavours are abundantly flowing.

My endeavours are abundantly flowing.

My endeavours are abundantly flowing.

I am a prosperity magnet.

I am a prosperity magnet.

I am a prosperity magnet.

How to make Your Own Affirmations

There are many approaches. Below are two.
No one size fits all. Find what works for you.

1.

A.
Think about what you really want in your life.

B.
Write as if you have it already.

C.
Keep it positive.

D.
Speak with conviction and emotion when you say it out loud.

E.g.

I attract abundance.

I am financially free.

I inspire love wherever I go.

I have a loving relationship full of joy.

2.

Ensure that they are rooted in truth, and are positive, practical, actionable and measurable.

A.
State what you are committed to and be specific.

B.
State why you are committed to it.

C.
State when you are committed to having it by.

D.
Speak with conviction and emotion when you say it out loud.

E.g.

I am committed to attracting more opportunities for my business by July this year.

I am committed to maintaining a loving and fulfilling relationship every day.

I am committed to having the best health by working out until the summer.

Have fun and find what works for you!

Create your own in the notes and / or share with me.

Notes

Notes

Notes

Notes

References

Gratitude Study

https://www.tandfonline.com/doi/abs/10.1080/10503307.2016.1169332?scroll=top&needAccess=true&journalCode=tpsr20

Science of Gratitude

https://bit.ly/scienceofgratitude1

https://greatergood.berkeley.edu/article/item/how_gratitude_changes_you_and_your_brain

Collaborative Research:
The Psychological Difficulties and
Benefits of Deliberative Reflection

https://www.nsf.gov/awardsearch/showAward?AWD_ID=1423747

The Miracle Morning - Hal Elrod

https://amzn.to/2VKbBWV

Atomic Habits - James Clear

https://amzn.to/3bvQsX6

The Biology of Belief - Dr. Bruce Lipton

..to/2Kqsxw8

ve Languages - Gary Chapman

.ttps://amzn.to/306kVGF

How To Think Beyond A Chart Position - Elroy 'Spoonface' Powell

https://bit.ly/5keyspoon

Printed in Great Britain
by Amazon